The Seminole Indians

by Bill Lund

Reading Consultant:
Tom Gallaher
Ah-Tha-Thi-Ki Museum
Seminole Tribe of Florida

Bridgestone Books
an Imprint of Capstone Press

Bridgestone Books are published by Capstone Press
151 Good Counsel Drive, P.O. Box 669, Mankato, Minnesota 56002
http://www.capstone-press.com

Library of Congress Cataloging-in-Publication Data
Lund, Bill, 1954-
    The Seminole Indians/by Bill Lund.
    p. cm.--(Native peoples)
    Includes bibliographical references and index.
    Summary: Provides an overview of the past and present lives of the
Seminoles, covering their daily life, customs, relations with the
government and others, and more.
    ISBN 1-56065-482-1 (hc)
    ISBN 0-7368-8056-9 (pb)
    1. Seminole Indians--Juvenile literature. [1. Seminole Indians.
2. Indians of North America--Oklahoma. 3. Indians of North America-
-Southern States.]   I. Title. II. Series: Lund, Bill, 1954-
Native peoples.
E99.S28L86   1997
973'.04973--dc21
                                            96-39764
                                               CIP
                                                AC

Photo credits
Cheryl Blair, 16, 20
Tom Gallaher, cover, 6, 12, 18
Index Stock, 8; M. Timothy O'Keefe, 10, 14

2 3 4 5 6 04 03 02 01 00

Table of Contents

Map

Canada

U.S.A.

Mexico

Where the Seminole used to live

Fast Facts

Today many Seminole Indians live like most other North Americans. In the past, they practiced a different way of life. Their food, homes, and clothes helped make them special. These facts tell how the Seminoles once lived.

Food: Seminoles ate corn, fish, and pumpkins.

Home: Most Seminole lived in a chickee. This is an open house with a palmetto-leaf roof. The floor is raised above the ground. Modern chickees have walls.

Clothing: Women wore long skirts and puffy blouses. Women also wore necklaces made of beads. They wore many necklaces at one time. Seminole men wore knee-length shirts. Today some Seminoles still wear special clothes. They have bright colors and many patterns.

Language: Seminoles spoke Muskogee and Mikasuki. Many still speak these languages today.

Past Location: The Seminoles lived in northern and central Florida.

Present Location: Now most Seminoles live in Oklahoma and Southern Florida.

Special Events: Some Seminoles still practice the Green Corn Ceremony. A ceremony is a special event.

The Seminole Indians

Seminoles have lived in the United States for hundreds of years. They have fought hard to keep their freedom. In 1957, the government accepted the Seminole Tribe of Florida.

Today 2,000 Seminoles live in Florida. Many live on Florida's six Seminole reservations. A reservation is land set aside for use by Native Americans.

Visitors to Florida often buy Seminole dolls and crafts. Seminoles also raise cattle and grow fruit trees.

Today many Seminoles also live on reservations in Oklahoma. Once these Seminoles lived in Florida, too. The U.S. government made them move to Oklahoma. But many still honor the Seminole way of life.

Today 2,000 Seminoles live in Florida.

The Seminole Home

Today many Seminoles live like most North Americans. Their homes are like most North American homes. But some Seminoles in Florida still live in villages.

In the past, many Seminoles lived in the Florida Everglades. This is an area of swampy land. A swamp is wet, spongy ground. It is covered with tall grasses and many slow streams. Seminoles formed villages on hammocks. Hammocks are islands of thick forests.

Seminoles built houses called chickees. Chickees are made out of cypress trees. The floor is a platform. It is about three feet (about one meter) above ground. Chickees have a slanting roof made of palmetto tree leaves.

Every family has their own chickee. The Seminole sleep in the chickee at night. Women sometimes work in the chickee during the day. It is also used to store things.

Seminoles built houses called chickees.

A Seminole Meal

In the past, Seminoles gathered together to cook and eat. The village built an eating house. This was the biggest house in the village. All meals were eaten there.

Women cooked together. They made food for the entire village. The regular meals were in the morning and afternoon.

A Seminole meal usually included fresh meat. Seminole people raised cattle. Many Seminole men were good hunters. They caught fish, turtles, deer, turkey, and other animals. The women cooked the meat for the village.

Corn was the main Seminole crop. It was used to make a corn drink called sofkee. Sofkee is still a popular drink among Seminoles on reservations.

Women made food for the entire village.

Green Corn Ceremony

The Seminoles respected nature. Taking care of the land was an honored duty. The Seminole religion centered around the Green Corn Ceremony. A religion is a set of beliefs people follow. A ceremony is a special event.

The Green Corn Ceremony was held every year. It celebrated the growing season. It also celebrated a new year and new beginnings.

The Green Corn Ceremony usually lasted from four to eight days. Women and men dressed up for the event. It was a time of dancing, games, and religious events. Every night, men and women danced around the fire. Women wore turtle-shell rattles. This kept the beat going. Men danced and sang.

Men did not eat anything during the Green Corn Ceremony. They drank strong teas. The teas made them throw up. They believed this cleansed their bodies.

Seminoles dressed up for the Green Corn Ceremony.

Clans

Seminole people belong to different clans. There are eight surviving Seminole clans in Florida. Oklahoma has some different clans. A clan is a large group of families.

The clans are named after things in nature. The clan names are Panther, Bear, Bird, Deer, Wind, Bigtown, Snake, and Otter.

Some clans break into smaller groups. Panther clan members sometimes call themselves Big Panther or Little Panther. More than half of Florida's Seminoles are Panther clan members.

Clan members are not supposed to marry people in their own clan. They are supposed to marry somebody from a different clan.

Clan membership is passed down from the mother. Each Seminole born becomes a member of the mother's clan.

Seminoles become members of their mothers' clan.

The First Seminoles

In the 1700s, Seminoles lived in Georgia and Alabama. At that time, they were known as Creek Indians. European settlers moved onto Creek land. Some Creeks moved to Florida to find new land. They wanted to hunt and live in peace.

In the 1800s, the U.S. government went to war with Creek Indians. The government wanted more land. The government won in 1814. Then even more Creeks moved to Florida.

At that time, Spain owned Florida. Spain wanted Indians to move to Florida. Spain gave them land. Many Indians also received horses and cattle to raise.

All Indians in Florida became known as Seminoles. Seminole means "wild people" or "runaway." Some African slaves became members of the Seminole, too. Slaves are people who belong to somebody else. They had run away from their owners in the United States.

Spain gave Seminoles land in Florida.

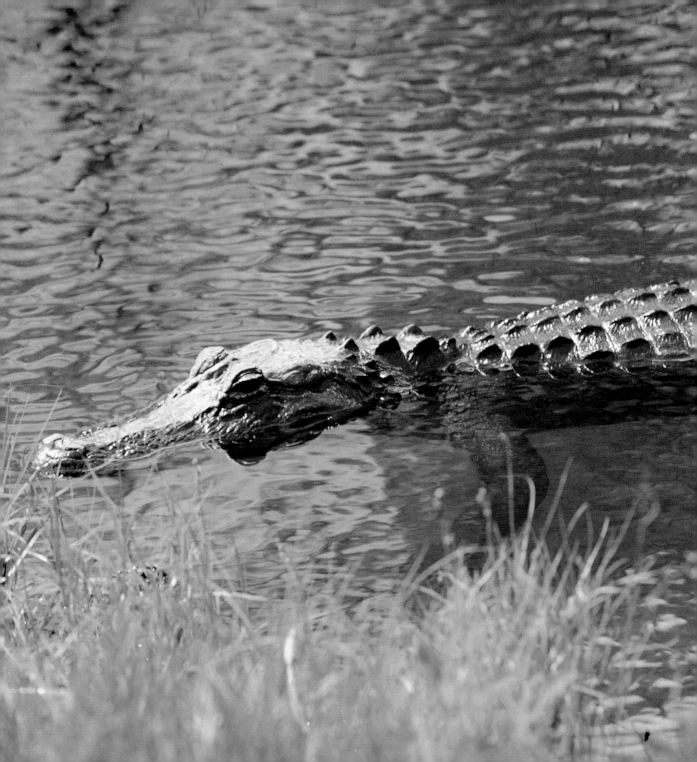

Seminole Wars

The First Seminole War began in 1817. Settlers wanted more land. The Seminole fought to protect their land in Florida. But the U.S. Army helped the settlers. It burned Seminole villages.

The U.S. government passed the Indian Removal Act. This meant the government could force Indians from their lands. The Second Seminole War started in 1835. The government tried to move the Seminoles. The Seminoles refused to leave. This was the longest and most expensive U.S.-Indian war. It lasted seven years.

The Third Seminole War started in 1855. People ruined Seminole crops and fruit trees. The Seminoles wanted to protect their land. They fought back. The war ended in 1858.

By 1858, fewer than 200 Seminoles were left in Florida. They hid in the Everglades. They planted crops and raised cattle. They also traded alligator skins and bird feathers.

In the late 1800s, Seminoles traded alligator skins.

How the Earth Began

Seminole people tell special stories called legends. Legends often explain things that happen in nature. One legend explains how the Earth began.

At one time, the world was covered in water. There was no land.

One day, a turtle swam to the top of the water. The turtle floated on the water. But he became tired.

The Breath Maker saw the tired turtle. He felt sorry for him. The Breath Maker gave the turtle a resting place on the water.

The turtle rested. He took deep breaths of air. The gulps of air made his shell crack. People came out of the cracks.

Once people were out, the cracks came together in squares. The cracks became streams. The people lived on the turtle's back. This is how the Earth began.

Seminoles tell how Earth began on a turtle's back.

Hands On: Play Stickball

Seminoles enjoyed playing games. One favorite game was stickball. Both men and women could play stickball. Now you can play stickball, too.

What You Need

A pole or tree that is 25 to 30 feet (seven and one-half to nine meters) tall

Masking tape

A tennis ball

Paper

A pen

What You Do

1. Tear off a piece of tape. Put the tape 10 feet (three meters) from the top of the pole.
2. Stand five feet (one and one-half meters) from the pole.
3. Take the tennis ball and throw it at the pole. Throw it as high as you can.
4. You get four points if the ball hits the pole's top. You get two points if the ball hits above the tape mark. Write the points you earn on the paper.
5. Each player gets five turns to throw the ball.
6. The winner is the person with the most points.

Words to Know

chickee (CHIK-ee)—a Seminole house; it has a raised-platform floor, no walls, and a roof made of palmetto leaves. Modern chickees have walls.
clan (klan)—a large group of families
Everglades (EV-ur-gladess)—large swamp area with tall grasses and slow-moving water
hammock (HAHM-uk)—an island of thick forest
sofkee (SOHF-kee)—drink made from corn

Read More

Garbarino, Merwyn S. *The Seminole*. New York: Chelsea House, 1989.

Koslow, Philip. *The Seminole Indians*. New York: Chelsea House, 1994.

Lee, Martin. *The Seminoles*. New York: Franklin Watts, 1989.

Sneve, Virginia Driving Hawk. *The Seminoles*. New York: Holiday House, 1994.

Useful Addresses

Ah-Tha-Thi-Ki Museum
HC-61, Box 21-A
Hollywood, FL 33024

The Seminole Tribe of Florida
6300 Stirling Road
Hollywood, FL 33024

Internet Sites

Native American Indian
http://indy4.fdl.cc.mn.us/~isk

The Seminole Tribe of Florida
http://www.gate.net/~semtribe/index.html

Index